STORY TALK 4

Sheila Freeman and Esther Munns

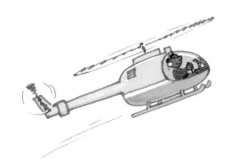

Nelson

CONTENTS

Picking up clues

If at first you do not see

Story talk

Celebrating story

Reading is a bit like going on a journey without moving from your chair.

Through books, we can travel to every part of our world and meet people whose lives may be very different from ours.

This book will help you to get ready for some really exciting reading journeys.

Be ready to pick up clues about people, places and ideas in your stories so that you can learn more about them as you travel together.

Our first book journey is *Around the world with John Burningham*. John Burningham, a well-known author and illustrator of picture books, travelled round the world in eighty days.

During that time he visited twenty-four countries and travelled 44,000 miles (70,500 km). He took with him a large sketch-book, a small camera and a tape-recorder. When he returned he used his drawings, photographs and tapes to help him write the story of his journey. When we look at the inside covers of his book, we get lots of clues about his adventures. Pages 6 and 7 can give you an idea!

In pairs, read and talk about all the information in these picture pages.
   Make a list of:
- countries visited and the dates given;
- different ways of travelling;
- names of some of the money needed on the journey;
- other souvenirs John Burningham kept to remind him of his travels.
   What reference books will you need to help you? Collect the ones you think will be most useful.

Have you ever made up a board game using ideas from a story? In small groups, plan a simple "Around the world in 80 days" board

4

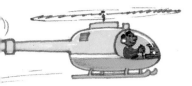
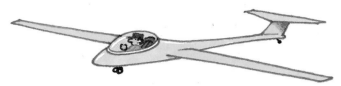

game. Use the information you have been working with. Talk about all your ideas first, and decide on answers to these problems:

- the shape of your board, and where START and FINISH are to be placed on it;
- what the rules are;
- what the rewards and penalties are going to be: for example,

one reward:

HONG KONG HILTON
Free meal
Go forward 3 squares

one penalty:

NEW ZEALAND
You develop skin rash
Stay put for 2 turns

- how many people can play the game at the same time. Look at other board games to help you with your ideas.

Design and make the other things you need to play your game, such as counters and a spinner.

Make a collage using tickets, programmes, menus, maps, photographs and advertisements to give a picture of life in the area in which you live. Arrange your collection in an interesting way before sticking anything down.

Look at your finished collage and tell each other any stories you are reminded of when you see the items you brought to school.

From your picture collage, what would a stranger to your area find out about:

- entertainment;
- transport;
- places of interest;
- shops and amenities (libraries, hospitals etc.);
- the different activities enjoyed by members of your group?

THE ICE PALACE

Some story journeys take us to worlds and people we have to imagine for ourselves. The best writers make such places and people come alive for us. Read this part of *The ice palace* by Robert Swindells to find out why Ivan sets out on his perilous journey.

Ivan and his brother lived in the house of their father the blacksmith, in a village in the shadow of the great, dark forest. The people of the village were poor, but in the summertime they were mostly happy, so that the pale, warm air rang with their laughter and their singing as they worked.

But as the short summers gave way to autumn their songs became sad songs, and their laughter thin. For they knew that far away to the north, Starjik was greasing the runners of his sled and rounding up his wolves. Starjik! Whisper his name and it was winter in your heart. Hissing over crisp snow in the black of night came Starjik behind his hungry team. Their eyes were yellow and their fangs were white. When Starjik was in a village the people lay very still behind their shutters but always, in the morning, a child was gone. For Starjik was known in every pine-woods village as the child-taker, and those he took were never seen again.

One night when an icy wind whined through the black

trees, and powdery snow sifted under everybody's doors, Starjik came to Ivan's house, and when Ivan awoke in the morning his little brother was gone.

All the village wept for the blacksmith and his wife, and for little Ivan who must now play alone. And little Ivan walked in Starjik's sled-tracks to the end of the village and stood there a long time, gazing into the north.

That evening, at suppertime, while his mother and father were not looking, Ivan took some of the dark bread from the big wooden board on the table, and slipped it into his pocket. Then he said, "Mother, I am very tired. I will sleep now." His mother lighted a candle for him and he carried the little flame into his room.

For a long time he sat on his bed, listening to the small noises his parents made beyond the door of his room, and to the wind outside. The wind made a sad, lonely sound, and as he listened it seemed to Ivan that something was crying out there in the night; something small and frightened that touched his window and moved away along the wall. And he lifted a corner of the window-curtain and pressed his face to the cold glass and whispered, "Wait, little brother. I will not leave you. I am coming."

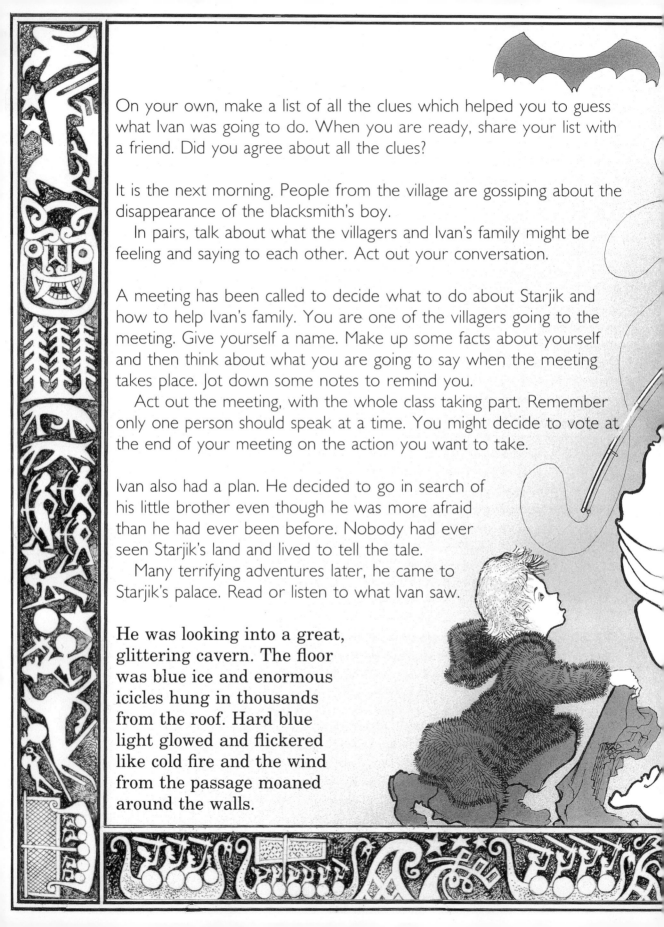

On your own, make a list of all the clues which helped you to guess what Ivan was going to do. When you are ready, share your list with a friend. Did you agree about all the clues?

It is the next morning. People from the village are gossiping about the disappearance of the blacksmith's boy.
  In pairs, talk about what the villagers and Ivan's family might be feeling and saying to each other. Act out your conversation.

A meeting has been called to decide what to do about Starjik and how to help Ivan's family. You are one of the villagers going to the meeting. Give yourself a name. Make up some facts about yourself and then think about what you are going to say when the meeting takes place. Jot down some notes to remind you.
  Act out the meeting, with the whole class taking part. Remember only one person should speak at a time. You might decide to vote at the end of your meeting on the action you want to take.

Ivan also had a plan. He decided to go in search of his little brother even though he was more afraid than he had ever been before. Nobody had ever seen Starjik's land and lived to tell the tale.
  Many terrifying adventures later, he came to Starjik's palace. Read or listen to what Ivan saw.

He was looking into a great, glittering cavern. The floor was blue ice and enormous icicles hung in thousands from the roof. Hard blue light glowed and flickered like cold fire and the wind from the passage moaned around the walls.

In the centre of the cavern, its back towards the boy, stood a hideous figure. It was stooped and crooked, and its white robe hung in folds from a bony frame. In one hand it gripped a thin, springy rod, of the kind which Ivan's people used to fish for trout in the river. As Ivan watched, the figure turned, pulling on the rod and watching something that fluttered and squealed far up near the roof, among the icicles.

It was then that Ivan saw what the man was doing, and his heart turned cold. Fishing! The creature was fishing, but not in the water, and not for fish. He was fishing in the air, and his victim was a tiny bat that whirled and tugged frantically as the man began to wind in the thin line. But struggle as it might, the poor creature was pulled closer and closer to its monstrous captor, and soon Ivan could see a streak of blood at its mouth from the cruel hook. When the terrified creature was close enough, the man clawed it out of the air, crushed it and dropped it on to the ice, where the broken bodies of several others lay. Then he threw back his head and laughed horribly.

Ivan drew back into the passage. The man's cruelty had sickened him, and the laughter turned his blood cold. He tried to tell himself that it didn't matter. The man had not seen him, so he could just turn round and run away and never see the creature again.

But deep within himself he knew the name of this monster. No other man could possibly behave with such cruelty. This man was Starjik and Ivan knew that if he fell into those awful hands, he need expect no more mercy than the poor, broken bat. And somewhere not far away, this creature had his brother.

In pairs, take turns to read aloud this part of the story again.

Write your own ending to the story, using all the information you have about the characters and the reason for Ivan's journey.

You will need to think about why Starjik stole the children, what he has done with them and what Starjik and Ivan say to each other when they meet.

Imagine that you have been asked to design a book cover for *The ice palace*.

Pick up all the clues from this passage to help you plan a cover that will make children of your age want to read the book.

Think about:

- what to put in the picture;
- the kind of lettering you would use for the title and author's name;
- the colours you would choose;
- how you would set out your drawing and lettering.

Share your planning ideas with the rest of the class.

Write a description of the cover you have planned, or draw and colour it.

CHARACTER CLUES – MEET MAD MARY

Maggie Blossom, her brother Vern and their grandfather Pap are out in the pick-up truck collecting old tin cans when they first see Mad Mary. In small groups, read this part of the story aloud.

Mad Mary was standing at the side of the road. She was looking at something in her hand, something she had just taken up from the road. She stuffed it in the bag she kept slung over her shoulder, and without a glance at the pick-up truck, she started walking.

Mad Mary was known for her cane – a long stick, curved at the top like a shepherd's hook. Kids were scared of that hook. "She'll grab you with it if you get close," they said, and they believed it. The cane moved like part of Mad Mary, an extra arm or leg. She was never seen without it.

"What was that she put in her bag?" Vern asked. He spoke in a whisper even though she was too far away to hear him. He had always had a dread of Mad Mary. If he was by himself when he saw her, he ran into the woods rather than pass her.

"I couldn't see. It was either a dead squirrel or a rabbit. It was too flat to tell."

"She'll eat it," Vern said. "She doesn't care what it is. She'll eat skunk."

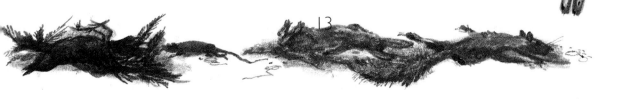

"Maybe she doesn't eat it," Maggie said, leaning back thoughtfully. "Maybe she just collects it to make potions and stuff, magic spells."

"She eats it," Pap said.

Maggie leaned around Vern to look at him. "Pap, people in my school say she's a witch."

"She's no witch. I went to school with her."

"You went to school with Mad Mary?"

Both Maggie and Vern were leaning forward now, staring at Pap. Both mouths were open.

Pap nodded. He steered the pick-up into a picnic area and pulled on the brakes.

"What was she like, Pap?"

"Back then I don't remember her being no different from anybody else," Pap said. "Except that her family had more money than anybody in the county and they always kept to themselves. Now let's pick up cans if we're going to pick up cans."

"How do you know she eats the stuff, Pap?" Maggie said, sliding out. The seats of the pick-up were worn as slick as a sliding board.

"We had a conversation one time. I was getting pop bottles – it was bottles back then. You got two cents apiece for them. I was walking along looking for bottles and I came on Mary. She was scraping something off the road. DORs she calls them, dead-on-roads."

"Gross," Maggie said.

"She thinks of it as dried meat – sun-dried meat. She said it's better than beef jerky. 'Course, most of the time she cooks her meat – varmint stew, she makes."

"Supergross," Maggie said.

"She invited me over one time."

"To her house?"

Pap nodded. "She was more sociable in those days. 'I make the best varmint stew in the county,' she said. I said, 'It would have to go some to beat my mama's varmint stew. It

15

was known statewide. You put red peppers in yours?' 'Red and green if I got them,' she said. We went on like that for a while, swapping recipes, and then she went her way and I went mine."

Maggie and Vern were staring at him as if he didn't have good sense. Finally Maggie shook her head in disbelief. "Pap, let me get this straight. Mad Mary invited you over to her house?"

"Yep," Pap opened a bag of trash in the first container and pulled out two Diet Pepsi cans.

"Where does she live?"

"At that time she lived in an old shack by the river. She built it herself, built it out of what was left of the old home place after it burned. Then she had to move when they put in the dam. After that she got less sociable, talked to herself instead of other people."

The children do not feel the same way about Mad Mary as their grandfather does. Find the clues which tell us how each person feels. Talk about them in your group.

Read this part of the story aloud again. Show how the different characters are feeling by the way you say their words.

Make a chart of what the children think about Mad Mary and what Pap thinks. Here are some headings you might use:

Appearance
Likes and dislikes
Personality

In this next part of the story, Junior, the youngest in the family, has been taken by Mad Mary to her cave. Now read on.

Mad Mary loved a good storm. It was the time she felt safest and happiest in her cave. . . .

Junior groaned in his sleep, and Mad Mary glanced over at the ledge where he lay. The noise startled her for a moment. She had forgotten he was there. . . .

The lightning flashed, lighting up his features, turning them white. Mad Mary waited to see if the lightning would wake him, but it didn't.

"I never saw a child that worn out." She shook her head, remembering the cruel condition in which she had found him. "Poor little thing. Maybe I ought to wake him for supper. He's probably starved. They never left him anything to eat but some raw hamburger."

She hesitated. "No," she said finally, "he probably needs sleep as much as anything."

Then she bent over her stew. Wonderful-smelling steam misted her face. It was done. She began spooning it out, ladling it onto an old pie tin. She balanced the pie tin on her quilt-covered lap and began to eat.

Outside, the rain poured and the thunder rumbled. Mad Mary forgot the storm. Mad Mary forgot Junior. By the flickering firelight she ate her varmint stew.

Talk about the clues you have found to make you change your mind about Mad Mary. Do you think she will hurt Junior?

Write an exciting end to this part of the story that will make children want to go on reading to see what happens next.

How many different endings were there in your class? Which ones were the most surprising, exciting, frightening?

17

HOW TO READ A POEM

Reading aloud and talking about a poem with a friend or in a small group is one of the best ways of enjoying poetry.

Here are some signposts to guide you.

1 Reading a poem can be like going on a mystery tour. Keep your ears, eyes and minds open

2 Always read the title. It may be a clue to what the poem is about.

Every poem has its own shape. Looking at the shape may help you to understand what the poem is about.

5

Take notice of punctuation marks; they are there to help you with the meaning.

4

Read the poem aloud lots of times. Be prepared to be surprised.

3

"The fight of the year" is the title of a poem by Roger McGough. In pairs, without looking at the poem, write down everything that this poem might be about. See how many different ideas you can think of.

Collect together the thoughts of your class before you read the poem.
  Now read the poem.

"And there goes the bell for the third month
and Winter comes out of its corner looking groggy
Spring leads with a left to the head
followed by a sharp right to the body
        daffodils
        primroses
        crocuses
        snowdrops
        lilacs
        violets
        pussywillow
Winter can't take much more punishment
and Spring shows no signs of tiring
        tadpoles
        squirrels
        baalambs
        badgers
        bunny rabbits
        mad march hares
        horses and hounds
Spring is merciless
Winter won't go the full twelve rounds
        bobtail clouds
        scallywaggy winds
        the sun
        a pavement artist
        in every town

A left to the chin
and Winter's down!
1 tomatoes
2 radish
3 cucumber
4 onions
5 beetroot
6 celery
7 and any
8 amount
9 of lettuce
10 for dinner
Winter's out for the count
Spring is the winner!"

Did anyone guess exactly what it was about?

For your second reading of the poem, one of you is the commentator on the fight; the other is the referee. The commentator sets the scene at the beginning, and from then on the shape of the poem will help you to decide which part of the poem each of you will read. Practise reading it aloud as if Winter and Spring are *real* fighters at a boxing match.

Imagine that this fight is taking place on television. Write what you want the commentator to say to the audience before the contestants appear in the ring. Build up a picture of Winter as a strong fighter challenged by Spring, a newcomer to the boxing world.

This poem is a splendid one for learning and acting out together as a whole class. In small groups, share your ideas about how the poem could be spoken and acted. Remember to include parts for everybody in your class. Jot down your suggestions and make a note of any problems you will need to solve. One person from each group should report back before you decide on final plans for your presentation. After your first practice, be ready to make changes if some of your ideas don't work.

TIME CLUES IN A STORY

The trouble with time is that sometimes it goes too quickly and sometimes it goes so slowly that it seems endless.

Do you have trouble with time?

   In pairs, talk about a time when you were enjoying yourself and you wished it would last longer. Then talk about a time when you were in trouble and it seemed as if it would never end.

The nine-year-old in *Time trouble*, a short story by Penelope Lively, makes a bargain with a grandfather clock to live again a bad Wednesday afternoon. He hopes to make a better job of it next time. Read about how it happened.

When I was nine I came to an arrangement with a grandfather clock; it was disastrous. Never trust a clock. Believe me – I know. I'll tell you about it.

   I was in the hall of our house, all by myself. Except for the clock. I'd just come in from school. The clock said ten past four. And I said, out loud, because I was fed up and cross as two sticks, "I'd give anything to have this afternoon all over again."

"Would you now," said a voice. "That's interesting."

There was no one there. I swear. Mum was out shopping and my brother Brian was off playing with his mate down the road. The voice came from the clock. I looked it in the eye and it looked back, the way they do. Well, they've got faces, haven't they? Faces look.

"I deal in time, as it happens," the clock went on. "Had some bad time, have you?" . . .

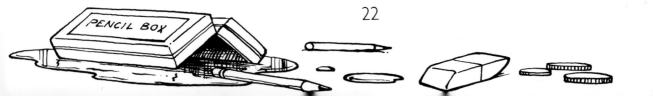

I nodded.

"Sometimes," said the clock, "I can lend a hand." It twitched one, from eleven minutes past four to twelve minutes past. "Tell me all, then."

So I told. About how at dinner I was in a bad mood because of having a fight with Brian and when Mum kept going on at me about something I kept thinking "Oh, shut up!" only unfortunately what was meant to be a think got said out loud accidentally so then Mum was in a very bad mood indeed with me and I got no pudding. And then on the way back to school Brian and I had another fight and my new pencil case got kicked into a puddle and all dirtied over. And we were late and Mrs Harris told us off. And I answered back accidentally and so she sent me to the headmaster and he told me off even more. And I had to stay in at break. And Martin Chalmers nicked my rubber so I had to keep asking for it back so Mrs Harris told me off again. And I had to go to the end of the classroom and sit by myself. And on the way home I got hold of Martin Chalmers and we had an argument resulting in me falling over and my pocket money dropping out of my pocket and ten pence getting lost.

"Tough," said the clock. "I see what you mean. Well – here's a deal. You have this afternoon back and I'll have next Wednesday."

"Next Wednesday?"

"Next Wednesday. Your next Wednesday afternoon."

"But I don't know yet what's going to happen next Wednesday," I objected.

"Quite," said the clock. "It's a risk. . ."

"O.K," I said. "And I have this one again?"

The clock made its whirring noise for quarter past four. "That's right, my lad. See if you can make a better job of it."

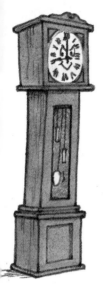

In pairs, make a Time Chart of the beginning of this story. We have started you off.

Time and place	Happenings	Time clues
Wednesday 4.10 p.m...?	nine-year-old boy talks to a grandfather clock about...?	"the clock said ten past four"
Place?		

Talk about all the things that could happen when the boy has his Wednesday afternoon again.

Write your own story of that afternoon. Decide whether it is going to be *better* or *worse* than the first one.

At the end of the story, the clock strikes another bargain with the boy. Read how this comes about.

"Tell you what. I'll be generous. I'll just have the time you waste. Now that you'll never miss."

I thought. I thought, I bet there's a snag somewhere. I didn't trust that clock an inch now. After a moment I said, "O.K. But just for next week."

"You're so sharp you'll cut yourself. A month."

"Two weeks."

The clock whirred. "All right, then. Done. Off you go. Have fun." . . .

And I was stuck with the deal. . . .

It was the worst two weeks I've ever had. I'm telling you.

24

Every time I stopped doing something, such as eating a meal or having a bath or doing maths or walking to school or getting dressed, everything just went blank. And there I'd be again in the middle of the next thing. It was like being in a speeded-up film. It was all go; there was never a moment's peace. I was exhausted. There I'd be cleaning my teeth and I'd dawdle a bit and try out a few faces in the bathroom mirror and then wham! I'd find myself downstairs and out of the front door on the way to school. Or I'd stop in the middle of a sum to have a bit of a think and the think would begin to get sort of vague and wandery – you know the way they do – and whoosh! there I'd be sweating away again at the sum and the bell would be going for break. I didn't know if I was coming or going. The only thing to be said for it was that the days went by double-quick. Suddenly the two weeks were over and everything slowed up and went back to normal. Goodness – what a relief! The first thing I did was go into the hall and stand in front of the clock and do absolutely nothing, for five whole minutes, on purpose. . . .

"All right," said the clock. "You've made your point." . . .

Look closely, then make a list of all the words and phrases that are about time passing *slowly* and *quickly* in the story.

Write a short poem about a time when "time" passed slowly or quickly for you. Use some of the words or ideas from your reading. Give your poem an interesting "time" title.

When a teacher or someone at home says "Stop wasting time", what are you likely to be doing or thinking about? Tell your partner.

Keep a Time Log for one day. Remember to keep a check on the time you "wasted".

BANANAS

Have you ever said or heard any of these sayings?

You don't understand what I mean.

Listen to what I'm saying.

But it isn't like that, it's different.

Maybe - perhaps... Yes - But - wait a minute.

Why don't you do as I tell you?

Look, try to see it from my point of view.

We aren't all alike. I don't think the same as you.

There's more than one way of looking at a problem.

You don't know what it's like.

The trouble is you can only see things from your point of view.

We say things like these when we want
other people to see things from our point of view.

All the stories and poems in this part of the book will help you to
look at people and animals and the things that happen to them,
from different points of view.

You may have to walk around in somebody else's shoes, turn
yourself inside out or even hang upside down from a tree to get a
new angle on the world!

Read this poem by Donna Wasiczko.

Bananas

It may be
necessary to hang upside
down from a tree
to get a new
perspective. Then you can
see that grass grows
up. What a dance
to measure lizard
jumps and spider
dangles at eye
level! To hear
birds fly
over your feet –
match shadows to faces,
feathers to wings,
footsteps to eyes.

In pairs, talk about the view of grass, insects, birds and people that you have if you hang upside down from a tree. What might you see, hear and feel?

Look at this diagram.

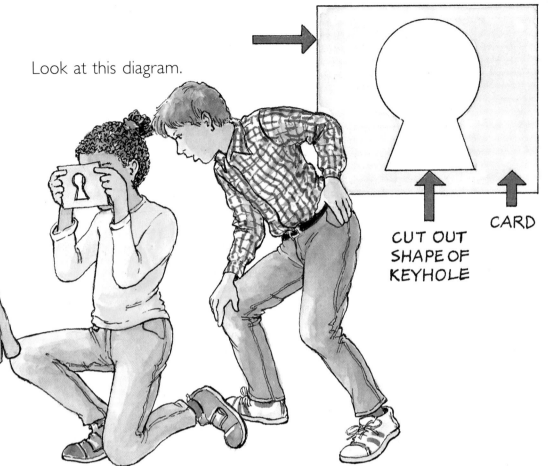

CUT OUT
SHAPE OF
KEYHOLE

CARD

Use the diagram to help you make your own viewfinder. (You could choose to make your viewfinder another shape.)

Find different places in your classroom to look at through your viewfinder. Describe to your partner what you see.

Talk about what your partner can see that you can't see through your viewfinder.

Take turns with your viewfinder as you move to different parts of your classroom.

You could also work from a sitting, kneeling or lying-down position to get a more unusual angle.

Use some of your ideas to write a short poem in the shape of your viewfinder.

I'M COMING TO GET YOU

In this picture book, *I'm coming to get you* by Tony Ross, a horrible monster from outer space is after little Tommy Brown who happens to be especially scared of monsters. We start the story where the monster found Tommy on its radar.

Imagine that Tommy could see the monster looking at him.
    On your own, draw or describe what Tommy saw.

Share your monsters with a partner. Talk about the ways in which your monsters look the same and any ways in which they look different. Now read on.

It was bedtime, and Tommy was listening to a story all about scary monsters.
The spaceship neared Earth, and the monster found out where Tommy lived. It circled the town, looking for the right house.
As Tommy crept up to bed, he checked every stair for monsters.
He looked in every place they could hide.
Once he thought he heard a bump outside his window.
The monster hid behind a rock, and waited for the dawn.
"I'm coming to get you!" it hissed . . .

30

In the daylight, Tommy forgot all about monsters, and he set off happily for school . . .
. . . but then with a terrible roar, the monster pounced.

In pairs, talk about your thoughts and feelings as you look at these pictures.

Tony Ross could have drawn just a big picture of Tommy's house. Why, then, do you think he drew all the other houses in the background?

Look closely at the two pictures together. Why do you think one is full of detail and the other is full of the monster?

Compare your drawing or description of the monster with the one in the story.

If you haven't already looked over the page . . . turn over now!

Did you feel surprised, disappointed, relieved, amused, or a mixture of all these feelings when you turned the page?

How does Tony Ross make us see things from the monster's point of view?

Make a list of everything in the picture which gives us an impression of the monster's size and strength.

This is the only picture in the story which does not have words to describe what is happening. Why do you think the writer decided not to use words?

Swap stories about any times you can remember being scared of something which was about to happen to you ... and your feelings when it did happen!

Write down one of your stories. Try to give it a twist at the end as Tony Ross did.

SMALL, SMALLER

Sometimes we only understand how small something is when we see it alongside something else. We didn't realise how small Tommy's monster was until we saw it alongside a matchstick and Tommy's shoes.

Russell Hoban's short poem "Small, smaller" says the same thing.

I thought I knew all there was to know
Of being small, until I saw once, black against
   the snow,
A shrew, trapped in my footprint, jump and fall
And jump again and fall, the hole too deep,
   the walls too tall.

Make a poster poem

Copy out the poem in your best writing on to a piece of plain paper.

On a larger sheet of paper, draw a picture of the shrew inside a footprint. Decide where on your poster to put the poem and the title.

In small groups, see how many more word pictures of smallness you can write using four lines – they do not have to rhyme. Begin in the same way as Russell Hoban.

I thought that I knew all there was to know
Of being small, until I saw . . .

Now try the same idea with *large, tall, thin*. On the next two pages are some photographs to start you talking.

AN ELEPHANT'S VIEW

Did you use the elephant as an example in any of your "Large, larger" poems?

In this next poem, "Elephant", Alan Brownjohn writes from the elephant's point of view. You might be surprised to read how the creature feels about his size.

It is quite unfair to be
obliged to be so large, so I suppose
you could call me discontented.

Think big, they said, when
I was a little elephant; they
wanted to get me used to it.

It was kind. But it doesn't help if,
inside, you are carefree in small ways,
fond of little amusements.

You are smaller than me, think
how conveniently near the flowers are,
how you can pat the cat by just

halfbending over. You can also
arrange teacups for dolls, play
marbles in the proper season.

I would give anything to be
able to do a tiny, airy, flitting
dance to show how very little a

thing happiness can be really.

36

With a partner, take turns in helping each other read the poem aloud. You will need to imagine that the elephant is speaking to a young child.

Make two columns on a large piece of paper.

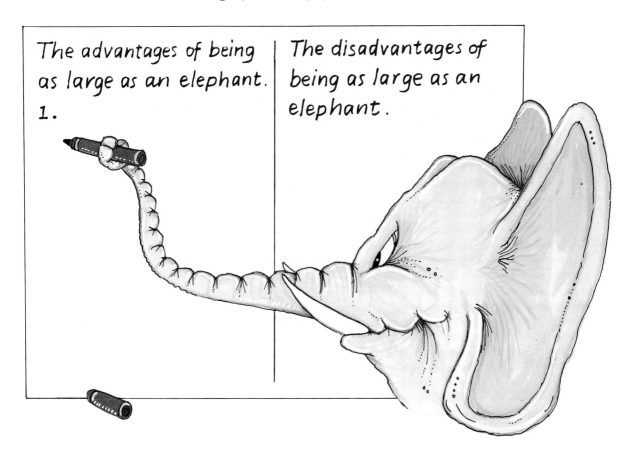

The advantages of being as large as an elephant.
1.

The disadvantages of being as large as an elephant.

Fill in the columns, using the ideas in the poem to start with, then adding ideas of your own.

Write a letter to the elephant. Try to convince him that he is lucky to be large. See if you can cheer him up and make him glad to be the size he is. You could point out some of the disadvantages of being small.

FIRST DAY AT SCHOOL

In small groups, talk about your first days at infant school. Here are some questions to help you remember.

- What did you think school was like before you went there?
- How did you go to school? Did you run into the playground or did you cling on to the person who took you there?
- What do you remember about your first classroom? Your first teachers? Your first friends?
- Did anything make you laugh or cry in your first few days at school?
- Do you remember your first Christmas at school?
- What is your best memory and what is your worst memory of being in infant school?

Read this poem "First day at school" by Roger McGough.

A millionbillionwillion miles from home
Waiting for the bell to go. (To go where?)
Why are they all so big, other children?
So noisy? So much at home they
must have been born in uniform.
Lived all their lives in playgrounds.
Spent the years inventing games
that don't let me in. Games
that are rough, that swallow you up.

And the railings.
All around, the railings.
Are they to keep out wolves and monsters?
Things that carry off and eat children?
Things you don't take sweets from?

38

Perhaps they're to stop us getting out
Running away from the lessins. Lessin.
What does a lessin look like?
Sounds small and slimy.
They keep them in glassrooms.
Whole rooms made out of glass. Imagine.

I wish I could remember my name
Mummy said it would come in useful.
Like wellies. When there's puddles.
Yellowwellies. I wish she was here.
I think my name is sewn on somewhere.
Perhaps the teacher will read it for me.
Tea-cher. The one who makes the tea.

Make a list of all the things the child is worried about or does not understand.

Write down three questions the young child might ask at home that evening.

What answers would you give if you were an older sister or brother? Think about how your first ideas of school have changed.

Plan and make a picture book for the reception class called *Your first day at school.*

You will need to gather information from the Headteacher, class teachers, school secretary, cook, dinner ladies, and children who were "new" last year.

Keep your drawings simple and your sentences short. Remember you want to make the new children feel happy to be with new faces in a new place.

NEW PLACES, NEW FACES

'It's all right. He's only a little boy, and it's the first time he's had to move. He'll settle.'

But James isn't so sure. The vast expanse of flat, boring fenland is anything but exciting for a young boy. And when he starts at the village school, it seems as if the bleakness of the land is matched by the hostility of the children.

But there's also the funny old man lying ill in the cottage next door. Gaffer Samson is his name and James likes him, although he doesn't know why. Gaffer asks him to seek out an old good luck charm, lost years ago – but helping out the old man will lead him straight up against the hostile school gang who cannot tolerate interference in village affairs.

'A deeply sensitive book, which ripples on in the mind long after you put it down' – *Country Life*

'At human level and plot level, it could hardly be bettered' – *Listener*

'Jill Paton Walsh knows where a child's real world lies' – *The Times Educational Supplement*

Cover illustration by Lynette Hamilton

Jill Paton Walsh
GAFFER SAMSON'S LUCK

Grand Prix winner of the Smarties Prize

We first meet James as he is travelling with his parents from the Yorkshire Dales to their new home in the Fens, twenty miles from Ely.

Here are two picture postcards. One shows a view of the Dales and the other a view over the Fens.

   Look at both postcards and then talk about what James would have found strange in his new surroundings.

Read the beginning of the story to see how he felt about having to move.

New places

"We can't be nearly there," said James, from the back seat of the car. " Here isn't anywhere. It's been nowhere for miles!"

"What do you mean, James?" asked his father, driving, with an edge to his voice.

"No up and no down," said James, "and no trees. Nothing."

"It's the Fens," his father said.

"But when we get there, Dad, please, Dad, there will be something, won't there? We're not going to live on this? Dad?"

"We're going to live where we can, James," his father said. "Belt up."

James looked out of the side window of the car. He saw ten level miles or more; no slopes, no trees, a green ditch on a black field, glinting red, as though ruled on the land with a Dayglo pencil, pointing straight at the setting sun, which glowered at him naked, just above the rim of the land.

His mother spoke to them both. To James she said, "There was no work for your father in the Dales, James. There's a good job in Peterborough."

"We could move to Peterborough. That's a place. There would be houses in the way of seeing this."

"We shall be near enough to Cambridge, too. There will be other jobs if this one folds."

To James's father she said, "It's all right. He's only a little boy, and it's the first time he's had to move. He'll settle."

"He must, we must," James's father said. "I don't like it either."

"We all will in time," his mother said. "Let's just get there."

But long before they got there, James was fast asleep.

He woke in a room full of light. He was lying under a white painted slope, which at first he thought was pink and gold;

41

then he realized it was reflecting very early light which shone softly on it through uncurtained windows. He was sleeping on a mattress on the floor, in his pyjamas, though he could not remember getting into them. His clothes lay tossed on one of three packing-cases standing at the other end of the room. It was a long low attic with a dormer on one side and two skylights on the other. The stairs came up in the middle of the room with a banister rail round them. James got up at once and looked out of a skylight. He could see a line of rooftops and a lot of trees. . . . James was pleased. This looked like somewhere. He could see between one tall tree and another a slender church spire a little distance off. Then he looked the other way, through the dormer window. A few new houses. A stump of brick – a windmill with neither roof nor sails. Just beyond it the plate-glass windows of what was obviously the school; and beyond that nowhere again. . . .

He sat down and considered the attic. He liked it, in itself. All it wanted was to be in Yorkshire, and he would have liked it a lot. He could put his stereo the other side of the stairs from his bed, and hang his model aeroplane from the ceiling. And if he put the bed under the skylight he would be able to lie on his back at night and look straight up at the sky. He tried it, lying on the floor, beside a packing-case, and at once saw birds skimming the roof, brushing the glass; he even heard the light dry scuffle of a wing feather. A considerable racket of birds was going on outside, he realized; perhaps that was what had woken him, rather than the light.

Then it occurred to him that nobody had promised him the attic. Perhaps it wouldn't be his; perhaps there was an ordinary room for him somewhere else. He had been too cross at moving to ask anything, or listen to anything about it. He picked up his shoes, and went down the stairs to explore.

Imagine you are James. Draw and write a postcard to a friend in Yorkshire. Say what you think and feel about the Fens and your bedroom. Remember there isn't much space on a postcard so think carefully about how to make it honest and interesting.

Share your postcard with a group. Talk about the different things your friends chose to write about.

New faces – James meets Gaffer Samson

In groups of three, read about how James meets the old man next door. One of you can read the storyteller's part. If you come from East Anglia you will be able to hear and copy Gaffer's voice. The rest of us get help from the way some of his words are written down. Help each other with the reading.

43

An old man was standing outside the back window of the kitchen, his back turned to James, seemingly just standing there, staring. James unbolted the back door and shot out through it.

"What are you doing in our garden?" he demanded. But he found himself standing on a gravel path, that ran the length of the long row of cottages, between the back doors and little fenced-off patches of garden.

"Oi'm not in your garden, though, boy," the man said. "Oi'm on the righter way. Oi've the right, you've the right, all them what lives in the whole row got the right. On foot or with a barrer to come and go by."

"Oh," said James. "Sorry. Isn't this bit ours?" He waved at the neatly planted little patch nearest to his back door.

"Thass mine, bor. Yew new in number two, are yew? Then thass your'n, over there."

James looked at a tiny piece of grass, all overgrown, . . .

"It's small, isn't it?" said James, sorrowfully.

"Thass not very big," the man said. "There's a vegetable plot goes with yours, down the path to the end, along of mine."

"Oh," said James. He trotted down to look. The path ran along the back of the row to a set of allotments at the end. James supposed theirs must be the one with nothing on it except dead Brussels sprouts. He trotted back. The man was still outside, staggering under the weight of a coal scuttle.

"Can I carry that for you?" said James. He looked properly at the man. He had big sagging features, and tousled grey hair. Little brushes of grey hair grew out of his ears. All his clothes seemed loose, and he stooped a little. He was wearing carpet slippers that bulged in shapes not much like feet.

"Oi dunno," the man said. "Can yew?"

James picked up the coal scuttle and carried it through the next-door back door. "Dew you put it down on the hearth, bor," the man said.

The room looked very old fashioned to James. It was all brown and cream and faded, and it had a bed in it, as well as downstairs things. He put the scuttle down on the hearth, beside the glowing fire.

"Thankee," the man said. "Now, wass your name, bor?"

"James. What's yours?"

"Mr Samson, I am. But everybody calls me Gaffer. Been called Gaffer for fifty year."

"Are you too old to go upstairs to bed, Gaffer?" said James.

"Yuss. Yuss, I am," the Gaffer said. "But I got enough sense to put me clothes on afore I goo out in the morning!"

"Oh, heck!" said James, realizing he was still in his pyjamas, and fled.

Talk about what James and Gaffer might think about each other after their first meeting.

Work together to plan a picture to go with the description of the old man in his room. Make notes about his size and appearance. Decide what furniture to put in apart from the bed. Think about the colours in your picture.

Draw some rough sketches. Work on one of them for your finished illustration.

New faces – James meets Angey

Read or listen to this part of the story. You will get to know more about James and you will meet Angey.

In your group of three, practise reading it aloud in an interesting way. Then carry on reading about James' first day at school.

Outside the big shop a small thin girl was standing. As James passed her she said, "Buy us a Mars bar."

James stared at her. "Why should I?" he said. She was wearing a T-shirt and a thin cotton skirt, and she looked very goose-pimpled and bluish round the lips, as one would expect, considering how cold a day it was. She was also very dirty: James saw a grimy watermark on her neck.

"I got the money," she said. "I wasn't asking for money. Just, will yer get it for me?"

"If you've got the money," said James, "why not get it yourself?"

She pointed at a card, neatly lettered in block capitals, stuck in the glass of the shop door. NO VAN DWELLERS, it said.

"That's me," she said. "They won't serve me, see?"

"Well, that's not fair," said James. The girl shrugged, and held out her money in a grimy hand.

"All right," said James, taking it. He worked his way round the shelves in the shop, with his mother's list, finding it all. Then he picked up a Mars bar, and queued to pay. Two women ahead of him spent ages talking to the girl at the till about the weather, so he took what seemed like hours to get out of the shop, but the girl was still waiting for him outside.

"You shouldn't eat Mars bars," he said, giving it to her. "They're bad for your teeth."

"Not if they're your dinner, they ain't, she said. "It's me dinner, this is. Can't be bad for me."

"It just is bad for you," said James. "You should buy something sensible for dinner."

"With 20p?" she said. "Leave off!"

"Oh," said James. "What does it mean, 'Van dwellers'? You can't live in a van."

"Mobile home, down the trailer park," she said. "Caravans. That sorter van. Course I can."

"Oh," said James again.

"I'm Angey," she said. "Who're you?"

"James."

"Visiting?"

"Come to live."

"See yer, then."

"I'll see you at school, I expect," said James, realizing as he said it that Angey might not be the best choice of first friend in a new place.

"Not if I can help it!" she said, skipping away suddenly down a narrow little path between houses.

First day at school

James stood a while near the fence in the playground. A game was being played on the tarmac between the school building and the road. It looked like catch and tag. James thought that was rather babyish, but everyone seemed to join in. He marched across to the crowd of children, and said, "Can I play?"

A big girl with plaits seemed to be in charge. "I don't know," she said. "Just moved here, have you?"

"Last week."

"But you're village, aren't you? This game is all estate."

"What's estate?" asked James.

"He can't be estate, Joanne," another girl piped up. "Nobody's moved out since last term. And nobody's moved in."

"That's the estate," the girl called Joanne told him. She

47

waved her arm at the houses across the road. Row after row of neat modern houses stood there. A line of council semis along the road, and behind them glimpses of the white-boarded and plate-glass fronts of newer houses.

"He could be from near Mark's house," a boy said.

"Are you?" demanded Joanne.

"I don't know where Mark's house *is*!" said James. "I've only been here a few days."

"There's a row of big new houses in the middle of the village, up Church Lane," she said. "Those count as estate."

"I'm not in one of those," said James. "I'm in a malting that was, just off the High Street, by the sweet shop."

"The Terrace," she said. "That's village."

"O.K.," said James. "So it's village. Can I play?"

"Not if you're village," said Joanne. "We don't like them, and they don't like us."

James shrugged, and plodded round the school building to the other side. There was another playground there, between the building and the open fields. There wasn't a game on this one; some little girls were chanting and skipping, and a little boy was bouncing a ball and counting his catches; the bigger children were all standing round in a huddle, talking.

James plodded up to them.

"No, you don't," said a boy half his size. "You lot play the other side."

"I'm not estate," said James. "I've moved into the terrace by the sweet shop."

The group parted, so that James could see a hefty big boy in the middle, smoking a cigarette. This boy stared at James from under a thatch of unkempt red hair. "Please, Miss, can I have more sums!" he crooned. "Strike a light!"

James said nothing. Then a little spark of anger suddenly made him say, "Any fool could do those things quickly."

"Who says we was trying to do them quickly?" the big boy

48

answered.

"Thass right, Terry, you tell 'im!" piped up a long thin boy in a striped scarf.

"You'll get us all set more sums, you will," a third boy said. "An' if you do, bor, we'll murder yer!"

"Just moved here last week, and thinks he's village," said Terry, shaking his head, and drawing languorously on his fag. "Thass rich!"

"How long do you have to be here?" asked James.

"Born here," a girl said. "You can't move here and be village."

"People must get born on that estate," said James.

"But you wasn't," said Terry, conclusively.

"Well, how long have *you* been here?" said James, returning Terry's stare. He was just a little more angry than dismayed.

"My family's always been here," said Terry. "I follow on."

"So what about Angey?" James asked, seeing her standing apart a step or so, back to the fence, looking on.

"Angey stops in our playground," said Terry. "And don't you go picking on Angey, or I'll fix you good and proper, Right?"

"I'm not picking on her," said James, "I'm just asking, that's all."

"Her great-gran come for the potato harvest in nineteen twenty-four," said the boy with the scarf. "Good enough?"

Once more the bell rescued James.

In pairs, one of you play the part of James, the other, his mother. Start a conversation between them like this:

Mother: How did you get on at school today, James?

James:

Mother will have to decide how she can help James to face the next day.

Then act out the conversation that James's mother had with his father after James had gone to bed.

Write it down.

STORY TALK

In this section you will meet lots of different kinds of story talk. There is the conversation between characters in poems and in stories. Sometimes you will be talking about stories you have enjoyed and how you can share them. Story talk can mean listening to what your teachers and writers have to say about the stories they have read and written. We can all get to know each other better through story talk.

TALK IN POEMS

Some of the most enjoyable poems to read aloud in pairs are ones in which two people, two animals or two objects are talking to each other. You may already have met some of these poems. If so, here is one more to add to your collection. It is a conversation between a mother and her young son. First of all, read it aloud in your head. It's by Brian Jones.

Banana talk

Bananas, said his mother, are curved and yellow.
They come in great bunches
like the hands of a gorilla.

Where do they come from? he asked her.

Jungles, she answered, where there are spiders.
The spiders are big and hairy
like gorillas' hands.

And do you like them? he asked.

They slide down, she murmured, pulpy-soft
and taste like pear-drops and scented wool.
They were my favourites.

And they're yellow? he asked quietly.

The skins are yellow.
They deepen blotchily towards brown
and they're ready to eat.

Do you eat the skins?

The skins are beautiful, she said, to look at.
But they're the worst part of bananas.
You peel them off, throw them away,
and what you're left with you eat.
It's white, and pithy-looking
like the inside of a conker-wrapper.

And what about the skins? he asked,
thinking yellow.

Men slip up on them, she said lightly.
And you have a good laugh.

In pairs, read the poem twice, changing parts.

It seems as if the child has never seen a banana. How does his
mother help him to understand how bananas grow, what they taste
like and what they look like inside and out?

Now read the last two lines of the poem again and then look at this
picture by Anthony Browne. The child probably thought his mother
meant something like the picture shown here. What else could she
have meant?

52

Here are some more sayings which have more than one meaning.

"It's about time you pulled your socks up."
"You are too big for your boots."
"Your eyes are bigger than your belly."
"Please lend me a hand."

Choose one of the sayings. Draw a funny picture to show one of its meanings. Write the saying underneath your drawing.

Talk about what else the saying can mean. With your partner, act out a short scene which could take place at home or at school. End your drama with one of you using the saying you have chosen.

Choose another fruit. Imagine that someone who has never seen it asks you what it is like. Plan your conversation poem. Use "Banana talk" as a model for your own poem.

You may have to write several drafts of your poem before you feel really pleased with your work. Don't forget to put in punctuation marks to help your readers.

Poster poem

Find a picture of your fruit.

Give your poem a title.

Write your poem out neatly on a large sheet of paper and decorate it with your picture to make an eye-catching poster.

STORY TAPES

Many short stories make exciting story tapes. Here is one for you to tape for the book corner. It's called *Why Anna hung upside down* by Margaret Mahy.

One day Anna, wearing her blue jeans, went out and climbed onto the first branch of the second tree to the right of the supermarket.

Then she hung by her knees.

She saw the world upside down. The grass was the sky and the sky was the grass. The supermarket poured people upwards into the green air.

An old man with a ridiculous hat came by.

"Look at this girl," he said to a thin woman with fluffy slippers and curlers. "She's upside down."

"My goodness so she is!" the thin woman cried. "Why do you think that's happened?"

"I don't know," the man replied. "Perhaps it's the weather, we've had some funny weather lately and it may be affecting the children."

"Perhaps she's doing it for health reasons," said a sickly

looking goat. "Being upside down lets the blood into the brain, and that perks you up no end."

A lion and a School Inspector going home from the supermarket stopped to look on curiously. The lion said nothing, but the School Inspector said: "It's the parents' fault. Parents let their children do anything these days. . . ."

"Yes, that's right!" called the mother of twins. "They don't care at all. Now if my twins were to go all upside down like that, I'd smack them with the hair brush. That'd bring them right way up again pretty quick I can tell you."

At this point, a boy called Ron, oldest of five, climbed up into the tree too and hung beside Anna.

"Look at that, now there's two of them at it," cried an excited voice, probably a hen. There were quite a few hens in the crowd.

"It's catching, it's catching," shouted the thin woman in fluffy slippers and the crowd moved back several steps nervously.

"I don't want to go upside down," whimpered a rich man. "All my money would fall out of my pockets. . . ."

"It's the new craze," said a folk-singing crocodile strumming on her guitar. Then she sang showing long rows of well-kept teeth:

> "Upside down – upside down –
> The newest craze to hit the town . . ."

But at this point a little girl called Sally wearing a track suit climbed into the tree and hung by her knees next to Ron.

"I still say it's the weather!" cried the man in the ridiculous hat.

"Now then," said a policeman coming up. "What's all this?"

"Look, look, the police have come," twittered some excitable guinea pigs, and a small number of culprits and criminals slunk away to evade the eye of the law.

"These poor children, neglected by their parents, have gone all upside down," said the School Inspector in an important voice.

"But perhaps," suggested a Professor of Philosophy going by with a meat pie in a paper bag, "perhaps they are the right way up. Perhaps it is we who are upside down."

This upset a lot of people. There was a resentful muttering and the sound of gritting teeth. The policeman had to do something quickly. . . . He thought hard.

"Send for the fire brigade," he commanded at last.

But the lion who had been watching thoughtfully, said in a deep lion's voice, "Ask them! Ask them why they are hanging upside down."

The policeman came up to Anna. "Now then, young lady!" he said, "why are you upside down in that tree?"

"I learned to do this yesterday," replied Anna, "I just wanted to see if I could still do it today."

"It's fun!" shouted Ron. "You all look funny upside down."

And Sally shouted: "Upside down frowns turn into smiles."

Then Anna put up her hands and swung down from the branch, and so did Ron and Sally.

"Why are you doing that?" asked the man in the ridiculous hat.

"Well, the bend of my knees is starting to hurt a bit," Anna said. "And not only that, it's dinner time and hanging upside down makes you hungry. Are you coming?"

There are seventeen reading parts including the storyteller. We have listed four; you find the others. Write them on a sheet of paper.

the storyteller   School Inspector
thin woman   excited voice (probably a hen)

In small groups talk about how you could turn this into a story tape.

You will need to share out the parts. Some of you will have to read two or three voices.

Think about each character and decide what kind of voice you could use.

Sounds of traffic noise and busy shoppers would make a good beginning and ending to your tape.

When you are pleased with your reading, tape-record your story.

Look back to page 28 to the poem "Bananas". Read it again.

You could write a few sentences to link it with this story and add it to your story tape.

Make a leaflet to advertise your story tape in the book corner.

Inside you could give some details about the author, Margaret Mahy, and other stories she has written.

List the names of the characters in the story, with the names of the readers by the side.

Write a few short sentences so that other children will want to listen to your story tape.

Design a cover for your leaflet. Here is one idea we had:

If you would like to read more Margaret Mahy stories, your teacher will tell you the titles of some of her other books.

TALKING STORY

You will get much more fun out of reading if you talk about the books you like with friends, family and your teachers.

Cheryl Thompson, a 4th Year Junior teacher, read this book, *Drift*.

Here is some information about the book from the back cover.

"No food, all lost," said the girl. "We die ever so soon." She sat on the trunk of a fallen tree. "No mans here," she said. "Land of bears, all ever bears."

Rafe the white boy had been forbidden to play with the "heathen" Indian girl Tawena. But when the two are swept on an ice floe into the heart of the North American wilderness, far from the settlers' village, only the girl's Indian skills can preserve them from the awesome danger they face. Can Rafe learn enough of Indian ways to enable them to survive? And why does Tawena disappear when they meet two Indian women?

Miss Thompson found the story so moving that she wrote a poem about it which she then read to some other teachers. They all wanted to borrow the book!

Here is her poem. Read it by yourself first and then aloud with a friend.

Spring ice
covers the lake
white boy, Indian girl
cross it
to see bear.
Ice breaks . . . .
cracks and strands them
on an ice island.

Superior
proud of his skills,
of his ancestors
who lorded this land,
white boy
goes to see bear,
sleeping bear,
on frozen lake.
Bear awakes!

Humble
knowing her land,
its woods and lakes
the way of bears
Indian girl
cannot read or write
does not talk
white man's language
stays with boy

Disaster strikes
boy humble
clumsy and faltering
leaves tracks in the bush
makes noises without meaning
like a simple minded animal
an ever mad bear

Disaster strikes
girl superior
swift and alert
shows courage and cunning
uses her knowledge
to ensure his survival
at one with her land.

59

With a friend, talk about the cover picture and the information on the back cover.

Pick out anything you have seen or read that would make you want to read this book.

Miss Thompson decided to read part of Chapter 14 to her class to get them into the story. Listen to it now.

After Rafe and Tawena had come on to dry land again, on to the firm ground, after the ice had brought them over the waves of the lake, after the hut had fallen all round them, Tawena was careless. But not careless enough to die.

It was easy to be careless. She had stood all night by the hot stove; she had known what happened when a brown bear put claws and teeth into a child, because she had seen it happen to a boy in camp. And she knew that whatever she did now, however she tried to get back to her own people in the village the far side of the lake, it would be very difficult with a wild boy like Rafe, who knew nothing about staying alive in the real world outside a house.

She looked at him now. He had no idea what to do, where to go, how to do it if he had known. He was tramping about on the lake shore, making noises, kicking snow and stone, waiting for things to come right for him.

"The white people do not think," said Tawena to herself. "Their faces are pale and their hearts do not work. He is, moreover, dancing like a bear." She looked round for the bear for herself. That creature had gone on down the shore of the lake. Now they were all on dry land it went away as soon as it could.

Tawena's instincts were working. She saw and heard many more things than Rafe did, looking and listening, watching and being aware, sniffing and smelling, feeling the wind and weather, searching the sky. . . .

She found a fire stone and asked Rafe for his knife. He did not understand what Tawena said, to begin with, and when he did understand he did not want to let her have the knife.

"Rayaf does not know that if we are together everything is for both of us," Tawena thought, but she could not say it, because Rafe would not know her words. "What shall we do," she wondered, "when I need the knife again to save our lives, and Rayaf will not let me have it? But then," she told herself, "I did not bring with me anything but my bare hands and what I know, and best of all, a little tinder."

When she began to make sparks into the tinder Rafe shouted at her.

"He is worse than a bear," she thought. "In fact a bear would have more sense than to make such noise. A bear is a wise creature and, if it knew how, it too would make fire. But that is a different sense."

Rafe seemed to understand slowly what she was doing. He began to look for fuel to burn, bringing out roots like stones, branches like rock, damp blocks of old grass. He stopped when she looked at him. It was no use talking to him in her own language, and she did not know enough of his to explain. . . .

"Rayaf," she said, to give him something to do, and because it might be useful, and because there might not be another chance for doing it, "get ever bit," and she pointed to the hut, where it lay collapsed in the water, partly rooted in ice, partly floating, partly shipwrecked on the rocks.

While Rafe looked doubtfully at the wood, which was still joined in large sections, Tawena heard something she did not want to hear.

She heard voices. She heard words she understood. Quietly, not far away, two Indian women, of her own kind, were conversing as they walked in the forest.

Bears were one thing. It is possible to go away from a bear. It is possible to frighten a bear away. A bear will forget you.

A bear does not want you dead; it does not want to kill you, though it will if it is hungry, or angry, and you are in its way.

But Tawena knew why she and her own family lived with the white men in the village, not with their own group in the swamps, prairies, and forests. They had dropped out of the tribe, because the rules were too hard for them to obey. The rule they had broken was to let Tawena live. There were too many girls in the tribe, and baby girls were not to live. Tawena had lived. Her mother had taken her to the white man's village. Because of that she was not marked with the cheek-cuts of those allowed to live, so Indian women, and men too, would kill her if she was found in the wilderness — though they dared not do so in the village.

Here, by the lake, there would be a quick blow with a knife of stone, and Tawena would not come home. Rafe, very likely, would not do so either. He would live, but only as a slave or servant among the Indians, being exchanged, perhaps, for some small useful thing.

"Rayaf," said Tawena, still listening, thinking that he would not fetch very much when he was sold because he was not good at useful tasks.

Rafe looked at her. He had heard nothing at all. It was as if he was old and deaf, like some dog fit only for stew, Tawena thought. She wanted him to make no noise, to put the fire out, to ask Maneto to send the smoke where it would not be smelt or tasted by the women. Tawena knew the smoke would be on the trees for days, and on the snow for weeks, perhaps, where any Indian could feel it with their fingers, never mind with tongue or nose.

Rafe made a noise. He said, "Hey," which meant he was about to speak.

"That is the way of the white people," Tawena thought. "First they make a loud noise with no meaning, and then they

say something that does not need to be said. Words are like beads to them; they wear them all over themselves."

Before Rafe managed to speak Tawena heard the Indian women taste the smoke and say the word for it. She heard nothing from them after that, and knew they would be coming to the fire. She told Rafe that they were coming, that she had never been there, that he would live with them, and must say nothing about her. She slipped away along the edge of the lake, through and among the bushes growing there, her feet silent under water-washed stone, her head carefully not shaking snow from overhanging branches.

From among rocks she watched.

Rafe followed her track for a little way and then could not see it at all. That meant nothing. It was likely that the Indian women could follow.

"If they follow," said Tawena to herself, "I shall not run away any further. I shall walk to them and give them Rayaf's knife, and with it they shall kill me. First I will tell them to take Rayaf back to his own village and perhaps tell my people to sing to Maneto for me. It is all in the hands of Maneto now."

Talk about what you have learned about the white boy and the Indian girl from this chapter. What is the "disaster" that the teacher writes about in her poem?

This chapter ends with a "cliff-hanger". This means that the reader is left wondering what is going to happen next. If you read the whole story you will find that most of the chapters end with a "cliff-hanger."

Find a "cliff-hanger" in a book you have enjoyed. Practise reading that part of the story aloud. Read it to friends and see if you can interest them in reading the whole story to find out what happens next.

TALKING STORY
WITH GILLIAN CROSS

Gillian Cross is a very popular children's author. If you have not met her books before, here is a chance to find out something about her and to read parts of two of her stories.

BIRTHDAY   Christmas Eve

ADDRESS   c/o Oxford University Press, Walton Street, Oxford OX2 6DP

SPECIAL VIRTUE   Listening to my friends (so they say)

SPECIAL VICE   Shouting at my children (so *they* say)

FAVOURITE COLOUR   Red – especially with black and gold

FAVOURITE FOOD   I like big thick stews, with lots of beans and vegetables followed by disgustingly gooey cream cakes

FAVOURITE MUSIC   Bach

FAVOURITE SOUND   A very fast train going through a station when I'm on the platform

FAVOURITE TV PROGRAMME   The Book Tower

FAVOURITE SMELL   Chrysanthemums

FAVOURITE BOOK WHEN YOUNG   *The secret garden*

IF I WASN'T AN AUTHOR I'D LIKE TO BE   A film director

AN INTERVIEW WITH GILLIAN CROSS

What was your favourite lesson at school?

English – especially when it gave me a chance to argue with the teacher.

When did you start to write?

When I was about seven. But it took me seventeen years before I managed to write a whole book.

How long did it take you to get your first book published?

I *never* got my first book published (and a good job too!) The second took three years, I think.

Do you set aside a certain time each day to write?

I write from 9.15 am to 12.15 on Mondays, Tuesdays and Thursdays and from 1.30 to 4.30 pm on Fridays.

How long does it take to write a book?

It depends on how long the book is. The *Demon Headmaster* took five months, but *On the Edge* took nine because it's more complicated.

Do you put real people in your books?

No. It would feel rude to me to use real people, and anyway that would take half the fun out of writing.

Are you writing a book at the moment?

I'm not sure. I *hope* it's going to be a book. At the moment it looks more like a jumble of scribbled notes. But my fingers are crossed.

Do you have any pets?

Not exactly. We've got some frogs and a goldfish that live in the pond, but it's such a big, untidy pond that we can't usually see them, so I can't be <u>sure</u> they're still there. But we had a lot of tadpoles in the spring, so I think there must be something going on.

Did you have a Demon Headmaster when you were at school? Sssh! He might be reading this at this very moment...

If you haven't met the "Demon Headmaster", you have the chance to do so now.

On her first day at her new school, Dinah is taken to see the Headmaster. She is led by Jeff, a prefect.

In pairs, read about Dinah's interview with him.

"The Headmaster will see you," he said. "Follow me."

Thoroughly bewildered now, Dinah walked into the school after him and along a straight corridor. At her old school, all the walls had been covered with pictures and drawings done by the pupils, but these walls were completely blank, except for a framed notice hung halfway along. Dinah swivelled her head to read it as she passed.

The man who can keep order can rule the world.

Frowning slightly, she went on following Jeff until he came to a stop in front of a door which had the single word HEADMASTER painted on it.

He knocked.

"Come in."

Jeff pushed the door open and waved Dinah inside, pulling it shut behind her.

As she stepped through, Dinah glanced quickly round the room. It was the tidiest office she had ever seen. There were no papers, no files, no pictures on the walls. Just a large, empty-topped desk, a filing cabinet and a bookcase with a neat row of books.

She took it all in in one second and then forgot it as her eyes fell on the man standing by the window. He was tall and thin, dressed in an immaculate black suit. From his

shoulders, a long, black teacher's gown hung in heavy folds, like wings, giving him the appearance of a huge crow. Only his head was startlingly white. . . His eyes were hidden behind dark glasses, like two black holes in the middle of all the whiteness.

She cleared her throat. "Hallo. I'm Dinah Glass and I –"

He raised a long, ivory-coloured hand. "Please do not speak until you are asked. Idle chatter is an inefficient waste of energy."

Unnervingly, he went on staring at her for a moment or two without saying anything else. Dinah wished she could see the eyes behind the dark lenses. . . .

Finally, he waved a hand towards an upright chair, pulled round to face the desk. "Sit down." He sat down himself, facing her, and pulled a sheet of paper out of a drawer.

"Dinah Glass," he said crisply, writing it down in neat, precise script. "You are being fostered by Mrs Hunter?" . . .

"Yes, sir."

"And why is she not here, to introduce you?"

"She couldn't come, but she's sent you a letter."

Reaching across the desk, the Headmaster twitched it out of her hand and slit the envelope with a small steel paper knife. As he read the letter, Dinah settled herself more comfortably, expecting to be asked a string of questions.

But there were no questions. Instead, he pushed a sheet of paper across the desk towards her. "This is a test," he said. "It is given to all new pupils."

"Haven't you got a report on me?" Dinah said. "From my other school?"

"No one else's reports are of any use to me," said the

Headmaster. "Please be quiet and do the test."

His voice was low, but somehow rather frightening. Dinah took a pen out of her pocket and looked down at the paper.

The questions were fairly hard. Mostly sums, with a bit of English thrown in and one or two brain-teasers. She knew that most children would have found them difficult to answer and she paused for a moment, working out where she was going to make her deliberate mistakes. Not too many. Just enough to avoid trouble.

Then she picked up the pen and began to write. As she scribbled, she could feel him watching her and every time she glanced up he was the same. Pale and motionless, with two black circles where his eyes should have been. She was so nervous that she stumbled once or twice, getting some of the answers right where she had meant to make mistakes. To keep the balance, she had to botch up all the last three questions. Not very good. It did not look as convincing as it should have done. Her hand trembled slightly as she passed the paper back across the table.

The Headmaster scanned it carefully for a moment, then looked up at her.

"You are an intelligent girl."

Dinah's heart sank, but, with an effort, she kept her face calm, meeting the Headmaster's gaze steadily. At last, he said, "But you make too many mistakes. I wonder –" He chewed for a moment on his bottom lip. Then he shrugged. "It doesn't matter. I dare say we shall find out all about you in due course."

She looked down to the floor, trying not to seem too relieved, and waiting to be told which class she should go to. But the Headmaster did not seem in any hurry to get rid of her. . . . Then, slowly, he reached up a hand to take off his glasses.

Dinah found herself shivering. Ridiculously, she expected

him to have pink eyes, because the rest of his face was so colourless. Or perhaps no eyes at all . . .

But his eyes were not pink. They were large and luminous, and a peculiar sea-green colour. She had never seen eyes like them before, and she found herself staring into them. . . .

"Funny you should be so tired," he said, softly. "So early in the morning."

She opened her mouth to say that she was not tired, but, to her surprise, she yawned instead.

"*So* tired," crooned the Headmaster, his huge, extraordinary eyes fixed on her face. "You can hardly move your arms and legs. You are so tired, so tired. You feel your head begin to nod and slowly, slowly your eyes are starting to close. . . ."

He's mad, Dinah thought muzzily. *The whole school's raving mad*. But she felt her eyes start to close, in spite of all she could do. She was drifting, drifting . . . All she could see was two pools, deep green like the sea, and she seemed to sink into them as she drifted off and off . . .

Talk about this Headmaster and why you would find him frightening, if you had to go and see him. Use some words and sentences from the story to explain your fears.

The problem for Gillian Cross was not inventing the "Demon Headmaster", it was deciding how to defeat him! This is what she says about it. **"When I'd finally done it, I swore that I would never write anything else about him".**

Fortunately for us, she changed her mind when she suddenly wondered **"What would the Demon Headmaster do with a**

computer – a SUPER-COMPUTER?" That was the beginning of *The Prime Minister's brain*, her sequel to *The Demon Headmaster*.

Dinah solves the Octopus Dare Computer Game and wins a place in the last round of the "Junior Computer Brain of the Year Competition". When she goes to London for the final, she has a feeling that there is something wrong. She does not have to wait long to find out what it is. Read on . . . .

Meekly Dinah let herself be ushered across to the empty desk and helped into the white lab coat that was hanging over the back of the chair. . . .

Nothing bad had happened yet, but still, at the back of her mind, was the niggle that had been troubling her for weeks. The feeling that there was something *wrong* about the final – about the whole competition. . . .

Almost as soon as she was settled the mechanical voice rang out over the room.

"The Computer Director Is Approaching.

Please Stand And Be Silent." . . .

Then, sharply, making them all jump, the sound of feet in hard shoes stepping out of the lift and walking across the floor.

A double line of men in white coats marched briskly up the room keeping perfectly in step with each other, not looking to the right or to the left. When they reached the front of the room, they spread out in an exact straight line, facing the desks, four of them on one side and four on the other.

In the centre, dominating the whole room, they left a space. *I won't look behind*, Dinah thought sternly. *I won't.* . . .

Then, from the entrance of the lift, a voice spoke. Very sharp and precise.

"Good morning."

Dinah stiffened. That voice! She could not believe that she had heard right, but now she did not *dare* look round.

"Now that you have all arrived," the voice said crisply, "we shall start work without wasting any further time."

Footsteps sounded as the owner of the voice began to walk up between the desks. Dinah hung her head so that her plaits fell on either side of her face, hiding it from anyone walking by.

No, she was thinking frantically, *no, no, no, it can't be true.* She was nervous and anxious and excited and because of that she must have made a mistake about the Computer Director's voice. She *must* have made a mistake.

But, all the same, she could have sworn that the voice she had just heard was the same as a voice she knew only too well. One that she had good reason to fear.

The voice of the Demon Headmaster.

In small groups, share all your ideas about how the story might continue and end. Remember what powers the "Demon Headmaster" already has and think about how he could make use of a computer to get into the Prime Minister's brain.

Choose your best idea and write the next part of the story together. Use this picture at some point in your own stories.

How many different endings to the story did your class think of? Which one did you like the best?

If you would like to read more Gillian Cross stories, your teacher will tell you the titles of some of her other books.

THE NIGHT TRAIN

Many of you will have grown up with stories, poems and jokes by Janet and Allan Ahlberg. Do you still enjoy reading any of these? Talk about the ones you remember with a friend.

Here is one amusing story, *The Night Train.*

Some years ago, when the world was smaller than it is now –
and a good deal flatter, come to that – the Night Train
brought the night. At the end of each day, it set off with its
loads of night – usually in sacks – and delivered them to the
four corners of the kingdom. (I should say the world was a
good deal *squarer* then, too). It also carried large numbers of
teddies and books of bedtime stories; toothbrushes, hair-
rollers and tins of cocoa.

Then, at each station on the line, sacks of night were untied
and the night itself rose up and enveloped the town (or
village, or whatever). Of course, as you will appreciate, night
came somewhat suddenly in those days. . . . The nights could
be patchy, too, and sometimes rather slow to fade away into
the following morning. Well, these were disadvantages,
certainly, as was the occasional sack of nightmares which the
Night Train also carried. However, there were sacks of sweet
dreams too, and by and large the inhabitants of the world (the
King, the courtiers, the loyal subjects) all found that this
arrangement with the Night Train suited them fine.

Then, suddenly, towards the end of a warm spring evening,
this happened: the Night Train was held up by a gang of
robbers (*dis*loyal subjects, you might call them), who robbed
the passengers, kidnapped the driver, and *stole* the night.

A few hours later a ransom note was delivered to the Royal
Palace. The King's secretary read it aloud to the King. "They
want a sack of gold for the driver," she said, "and half your
kingdom for the night."

"Half my kingdom?" cried the King. "That's daylight robbery!"

"It's traditional, though," his secretary said.

Meanwhile, in both halves of the kingdom there was much
yawning and scratching of heads. Night-club owners were
looking worried, night-school teachers were twiddling their

thumbs, and the palace switchboard was jammed with calls from irate parents unable to get their children off to bed.

Well, the next day – or rather the *same* day, for the sun was still low in the sky – the King called an emergency meeting of the Royal Council together with his Chief of Police.

During the meeting, the Archbishop said, "I believe the day of reckoning is at hand!"

The Royal Philosopher said, "The longest day must have an end." And (a little later), "Tomorrow is another day!"

The Chief of Police said, "We are searching for those robbers night and day . . . well, *day* anyway."

And the King's Doctor said, "An apple a day keeps the doctor away," which was what he usually said.

After the meeting – which reached no useful conclusion – the King continued to discuss the matter with his secretary. Her advice was straightforward. "Issue a Royal Proclamation," she said. "Have it proclaimed throughout the length and breadth of the land."

"The land's square," said the King. "The length and breadth are the same."

"Don't quibble," said his secretary. "Offer half your kingdom –"

"Not that again," said the King.

"And the hand of your daughter in marriage, to whosoever –"

"I don't *have* a daughter," said the King. "I'm not even married!"

"Never mind," said his secretary, firmly. "It's traditional."

Now then, whether the King would have taken this advice, I have to confess will never be known. For at this point in the story we have come to a sort of right turn, as it were. You see, it is also traditional in stories involving sacks (ropes and nets, too, I believe) for *mice* to play a part. What invariably happens is, they nibble through the hero's bonds, or the net in which the lion has been captured, or – as in this case – one of the sacks of night piled up in the robbers' hideout.

Well, I've no doubt you can guess what happened next. For one thing, the hideout was not a hideout for long. Soon, hanging over it like a marker buoy, there was a small patch of dark and starry sky. (The night had poured out of the sack, you see, and escaped up the chimney.)

So then the police surrounded the place; the robbers gave themselves up; the sacks of night were loaded once more onto the Night Train, and life, in hardly any time at all, returned to normal. In the days (or rather nights) that followed, there was once more employment for night-watchmen, overtime for railway-workers and a good night's sleep for anyone who wanted it. There again, those that chose to make a night of it were free to do so; ships that wanted to pass in the night could pass in the night, and things that went *bump* in the night could . . . bump.

So there we are: what else can I tell you? Well, the robbers were sent to jail for a thousand and one nights (and days), and the King in due course married his secretary. They had grown extremely fond of each other, and besides, as the King explained when he proposed, it was traditional.

As for the Night Train, it continued to give good service for many years, until, by and by, the telescope was invented and scientists discovered the movement of the planets. The world, it turned out, wasn't square at all, but round like an orange. Furthermore, it "rotated on its axis" (whatever that means) every twenty-four hours, causing night to follow day . . . *automatically.* (I may say, quite a few people fell *off* the earth when first they heard how fast it was spinning, and many more went about on their hands and knees for weeks.)

However, progress will not be denied, I suppose, and sure enough from that time on the Night Train was done for. Now it lies rusting and forgotten in a siding, the King's great-granddaughter rules the land and the *Gravy* Train is all the

rage. Of course, it carries rather more than gravy, you understand. I mean, what use is gravy without lamb chops, for instance, and mint sauce, and roast potatoes and peas and baby carrots? And what's a dinner without a pudding: deep-dish apple pie and cinnamon and cream – and what's a pudding without . . . ? But there we are, I'm getting carried away and will be into another story soon, if I don't watch it. "The longest day must have an end," as the Royal Philosopher said, and the longest story, too, if it comes to that. So, I will stop now, desist, lay down my pen, and call it a day . . . Well, all right, a "*night*" then.

In pairs, talk about any part of the story that made you laugh.

Make a list of the sayings in the story that have two meanings. Guess or find out what they mean.

When you know what the "Gravy Train" means, write a funny story about it. Here are some more sayings you might like to use:

"He has missed the boat."
"He has hit the jackpot."
"He has chanced his arm."

DIDN'T YOU KNOW HOW FRIGHTENED I WAS?

Tell your partner stories about times when you were afraid. They could be about

- being lost;
- the dark;
- a dare;
- trying something hard for the first time;
- telling a lie;
- an accident;
- something that made you jump, for example, a mouse;
- being away from home;
- anything else that has happened to you.

Did any of the other people in your story know how frightened *you* were?

In this poem "The fieldmouse's monologue", by Elizabeth Jennings, a fieldmouse is frightened by a human being. And the human is afraid of the mouse. The fieldmouse tells the story of how it happened.

Didn't you know how frightened I was when I came
For shelter in your room? I am not tame.
You looked enormous when I saw you first.
I rushed to the hole I had made, took refuge there,
Crouched behind paper you thrust at me, shivered with fear.
I had smelt some chocolate. The kitchen was warm below
And outside there was frost and, one whole night, great snow.

I only guessed you were frightened too when you
Called out loudly, deafeningly to me.
My ears are small but my hearing strong, you see.
You pushed old papers against my hole and so
I had to climb into a drawer. You did not know
That I could run so high. I felt your hand,
Like my world in shadow, shudder across me and
I scuttled away but felt a kind of bond
With you in your huge fear.
Was I the only friend near?

Write the story that the fieldmouse might have told his family when
he got back to his nest.

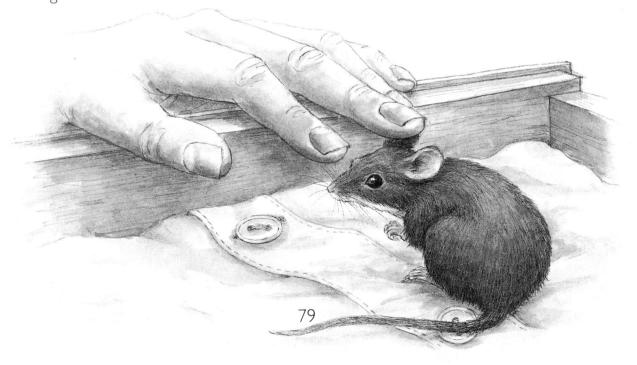

79

A DAY TO REMEMBER

Have you ever seen young children jump from a high place into the arms of a grown-up waiting to catch them? They do it again and again and enjoy the excitement and the danger. They know they are safe!

Keep this in your minds as you read about Mary's daring ride on a weathercock at the top of a new church that her father was building. On this special day she has climbed up to the spire of St Philip's to take him some food. Read the story aloud in pairs. It's from *The stone book* by Alan Garner.

Mary stood and looked out from the spire. "And the church," she said. "It's so far away." She knelt and squinted between the planks. "The roof's as far as the ground. We're flying."

Father watched her; his combing hammer swung from his arm.

"There's not many who'll be able to say they've been to the top of Saint Philip's."

"But I'm not at the top," said Mary.

The steeple cap was a swelling to take the socket for the spike of the golden cockerel. Mary could touch the spike. Above her the smooth belly raced the clouds.

"You're not frit?"

"Not now," said Mary. "It's grand."

Father picked her up. "You're really not frit? Nobody's been that high. It was reared from the platform."

"Not if you help me," said Mary.

"Right," said Father. "He could do with a testing. Let's see if he runs true."

Father lifted Mary in his arms, thick with work from wrist to elbow. For a moment again the steeple wasn't safe on the earth when she felt the slippery gold of the weathercock bulging over her, but she kicked her leg across its back, and held the neck.

"Get your balance," said Father.

"I've got it," said Mary.

The swelling sides were like a donkey, and behind her the tail was stiff and high. Father's head was at her feet, and he could reach her.

"I'm set," she said.

Father's face was bright and his beard danced. He took off his cap and swept it in a circle and gave the cry of the summer fields.

"Who-whoop! Wo-whoop! Wo-o-o-o!"

Mary laughed. The wind blew on the spire and made the weathercock seem alive. The feathers of its tail were a marvel.

Father twisted the spike with his hands against the wind, and the spike moved in its greased socket, shaking a bit, juddering, but firm. To Mary the weathercock was waking. The world turned. Her bonnet fell off and hung by its ribbon, and the wind filled her hair.

"Faster! Faster!" she shouted. "I'm not frit!" She banged her heels on the golden sides, and the weathercock boomed.

"Who-whoop! Wo-whoop! Wo-o-o-o!" cried Father. The high note of his voice crossed parishes and townships. Her hair and her bonnet flew, and she felt no spire, but only the brilliant gold of the bird spinning the air.

Father swung the tail as it passed him. "Who-whoop! Wo-whoop! Wo-o-o-o! There's me tip-top pickle of the corn!"

Mary could see all of Chorley, the railway and the new houses. She could have seen home but the Wood Hill swelled and folded into Glaze Hill between. She could see the cottage at the edge of Lifeless Moss, and the green of the Moss, and as she spun she could see Lord Stanley's, and Stockport and Wales, and Beeston and Delamere, and all to the hills and Manchester. The golden twisting spark with the girl on top, and everywhere across the plain were churches.

"Churches! I can see churches!"

And all the weathercocks turned in the wind.

Father let the spike stop, and lifted her down.

"There," he said. "You'll remember this day, my girl. For the rest of your life."

"I already have," said Mary.

Why do you think Mary will always remember this day?
    What will she tell her mother about it when she gets back home?

Tell or write your own story about "A day to remember".

THERE CAME A DAY

Imagine that summer becomes autumn in one day!

Talk about and write down the changes that would have to take place to make this happen.

What would happen to:

- the trees;
- the sun;
- the birds;
- the seeds;
- the people?

Read what Ted Hughes imagined when he wrote this poem.

There came a day that caught the summer
Wrung its neck
Plucked it
And ate it.

Now what shall I do with the trees?
The day said, the day said.
Strip them bare, strip them bare.
Let's see what is really there.

And what shall I do with the sun?
The day said, the day said.
Roll him away till he's cold and small.
He'll come back rested if he comes back at all.

And what shall I do with the birds?
The day said, the day said.
The birds I've frightened, let them flit,
I'll hang out pork for the brave tomtit.

83

And what shall I do with the seed?
The day said, the day said.
Bury it deep, see what it's worth.
See if it can stand the earth.

What shall I do with the people?
The day said, the day said.
Stuff them with apple and blackberry pie –
They'll love me then till the day they die.

There came this day and he was autumn.
His mouth was wide
And red as a sunset.
His tail was an icicle.

In small groups, or as a whole class, prepare this poem to read aloud.
    Decide which lines should be said by one voice, which ones by a small group of voices and which by the whole class.

Write your own group poem called "There came a day". It could be about a day when:
- winter becomes spring;
- spring becomes summer;
- autumn becomes winter.

    Use the questions Ted Hughes asks in his poem to help you with your writing.
    Copy out your best effort. Illustrate it if you wish and share it with the rest of the class.

THE BANANA TREE

Sudden changes in the weather can take place without very much warning. Some of you will have stories to tell about the hurricane which came during the morning of 16th October, 1987. It killed people, and destroyed property and millions of trees in the southern part of England.

In some parts of the world, hurricanes happen more often. In this story of courage, Gustus Bass, a young Jamaican boy, and his family are huddled together in the schoolroom. They had fled there with other villagers when the storm broke. We take up the story at this point. Read it or listen to it being read to you. It's from *The banana tree* by James Berry.

. . . the wind outside mocked viciously. It screamed. It whistled. It smashed everywhere up.

Mrs Bass had tightly closed her eyes, singing and swaying in the centre of the children who nestled round her. But Gustus was by himself. He had his elbows on his knees and his hands blocking his ears. He had his own worries.

What's the good of Pappy asking all those questions when he treat him so bad. He's the only one in the family without a pair of shoes! Because he's a big boy he dohn need anythin' an' must do all the work. He can't stay at school in the evenings an' play cricket because there's work to do at home. He can't have no outings with the other children because he has no shoes. An' now when he was to sell his bunch of bananas an' buy shoes so he can go out with his cricket team, the hurricane is going to blow it down.

It was true: the root of the banana was his "navel string". After his birth the umbilical cord was dressed with castor oil

85

and sprinkled with nutmeg and buried, with the banana tree planted over it for him. When he was nine days old the Nana midwife had taken him out into the open for the first time. She had held the infant proudly and walked the twenty-five yards that separated the house from the kitchen, and at the back showed him his tree. "'Memba w'en you grow up," her toothless mouth had said, "It's you nable strings feedin' you tree, the same way it feed you from you mudder."

Refuse from the kitchen made the plant flourish out of all proportion. But the rich soil around it was loose. Each time the tree gave a shoot, the bunch would be too heavy for the soil to support; so it crashed to the ground, crushing the tender fruit. This time, determined that his banana must reach the market, Gustus had supported his tree with eight props. And watching it night and morning it had become very close to him. . . .

Muffled cries, and the sound of blowing noses, now mixed with the singing. Delayed impact of the disaster was happening. Sobbing was everywhere. . . .

Realising that his family, too, was overwhelmed by the surrounding calamity, Mr Bass bustled over to them. Because their respect for him bordered fear, his presence quietened all immediately. He looked round. "Where's Gustus! Imogene . . . where's Gustus!"

"He was 'ere, Pappy," she replied, drying her eyes. "I dohn know when he get up."

Briskly, Mr Bass began combing the schoolroom to find his boy. He asked; no one had seen Gustus. He called. There was no answer. . . .

By this time Gustus was half-way on the mile journey to their house. The lone figure in the raging wind and shin-deep road-flood was tugging, snapping and pitching branches out of his path. His shirt was fluttering from his back like a boat-

sail. . . . As he grimaced and covered his ears he was forcefully slapped against a coconut tree trunk that laid across the road.

When his eyes opened, his round face was turned up to a festered sky. Above the tormented trees a zinc sheet writhed, twisted and somersaulted in the tempestuous flurry. . . . As Gustus turned to get up, a bullet-drop of rain struck his temple. He shook his head, held grimly to the tree trunk and struggled to his feet. . . .

When Gustus approached the river he had to cross, it was flooded and blocked beyond recognition. . . . The wrecked footbridge had become the harbouring fort for all the debris, branches and monstrous tree-trunks which the river swept along its course. The river was still swelling. More accumulation arrived each moment, ramming and pressing the bridge. Under pressure it was cracking and shifting minutely towards a turbulent forty-foot fall.

Gustus had seen it! A feeling of dismay paralysed him, reminding him of his foolish venture. . . . But how can he go back. He has no strength to go back. His house is nearer than the school. An' Pappy will only strap him for nothin' . . . for nothin' . . . no shoes, nothin' when the hurricane is gone. . . .

He made a bold step and the wind half-lifted him, ducking him in the muddy flood. He sank to his neck. Floating leaves, sticks, coconut husks, dead ratbats and all manner of feathered creatures and refuse surrounded him. . . . But he struggled desperately until he clung to the laden bridge, and climbed up among leafless branches. . . .

The urgency of getting across became more frightening, and he gritted his teeth and dug his toes into the debris, climbing with maddened determination. . . .

There was a powerful jolt. Gustus flung himself into the air and fell in the expanding water on the other side. When he surfaced, the river had dumped the entire wreckage into the gurgling gully. For once the wind helped. It blew him to land.

Gustus was in a daze when he reached his house. Mud and rotten leaves covered his head and face, and blood caked around a gash on his chin. . . .

He could hardly recognise his yard. The terrorised trees that stood were writhing in turmoil. Their thatched house had collapsed like an open umbrella that was given a heavy blow. He looked the other way and whispered, "Is still dere! Dat's a miracle. . . . Dat's a miracle."

Dodging the wind, he staggered from tree to tree until he got to his own tormented banana tree. Gustus hugged the tree. "My nable string!" he cried. "My nable string! I know you would stan' up to it, I know you would."

The bones of the tree's stalky leaves were broken, and the wind lifted them and harrassed them. And over Gustus's head the heavy fruit swayed and swayed. The props held the tree, but they were squeaking and slipping. And around the plant the roots stretched and trembled, gradually surfacing under loose earth.

With the rags of his wet shirt flying off his back, Gustus was down busily on his knees, bracing, pushing, tightening the props. One by one he was adjusting them until a heavy rush of wind knocked him to the ground. A prop fell on him, but he scrambled to his feet and looked up at the thirteen-hand bunch of bananas. "My good tree," he bawled, "hol' yo' fruit . . . keep it to yo' heart like a mudder savin' her baby! Dohn let the wicked wind t'row you to the groun' . . . even if it t'row me to the groun'. I will not leave you."

But several attempts to replace the prop were futile. . . . . The wind tossed him, like washing on the line, against his tree. . . . .

As darkness began to move in rapidly, the wind grew more vicious and surged a mighty gust which struck the resisting kitchen. It was heaved to the ground in a rubbled pile. The brave wooden hut had been shielding the banana tree, but in its death-fall missed it by inches. The wind charged again and

the soft tree gurgled – the fruit was torn from it and plunged to the ground.

The wind was less fierce when Mr Bass and a searching-party arrived with lanterns. Because the bridge was washed away, the hazardous roundabout journey had badly impeded them.

Talks about safety were mockery to the anxious father. Relentlessly he searched. In the darkness his great voice echoed everywhere, calling for his boy. He was wrenching and ripping through the house wreckage when suddenly he vaguely remembered how the boy had been fussing with the banana tree. Desperate, the man struggled from the ruins, flagging the lantern he carried.

The flickering light above his head showed Mr Bass the forlorn and pitiful banana tree. . . . Half of the damaged fruit rested on Gustus. The father hesitated. But when he saw a feeble wink of the boy's eyelids he flung himself to the ground. . . . "My bwoy!" he murmured. "Mi hurricane bwoy! The Good Lord save you. . . . Why you do this? Why you do this?"

"I did wahn buy mi shoes, Pappy. I . . . I cahn go anywhere 'cause I have no shoes. . . . I didn' go to school outing at the factory. I didn' go to Government House. I didn' go to Ol' Fort in town."

Mr Bass sank into the dirt and stripped himself of his heavy boots. He was about lacing them to the boy's feet when the onlooking men prevented him. He tied the boots together and threw them over his shoulder.

Gustus's broken arm was strapped to his side as they carried him away. Mr Bass stroked his head and asked how he felt. Only then, grief swelled inside him and he wept.

You will find other stories by James Berry in this book.

Tell each other any true stories you have heard about children who have shown great courage. Bring in newspaper stories and pictures to make a display in your classroom.

THE STORY OF CHRISTMAS

All over the world, people hold festivals to celebrate important occasions in the year.

One of the most joyful festivals for children celebrates the story of Christmas.

The poet, Charles Causley, has written a verse play about the story of Christmas. He called it *The gift of a lamb*. In his play you will meet these ten characters.

Storyteller	1st Angel
Ben, the grandfather	2nd Angel
John, the son } shepherds	3rd Angel
Dan, the grandson	Joseph
Thieving Jack	Mary

On a cold winter's night, long ago, three shepherds sit on a hill watching their sheep. Young Dan is especially excited, for at midnight it is his birthday and he can pick the first lamb to start his own flock. The little black and white lamb he has chosen also catches the eye of the notorious Thieving Jack, who is creeping nearer and nearer . . .

[*What at first seems to be a rock or boulder slowly begins to move. It is* THIEVING JACK. *The shepherds' music is heard a little distance off, and held behind his voice as he begins to speak.*]

THIEVING   Hark to the silly shepherds
JACK: As they sing and as they play –
             Though what they've got to sing about
             Is more than I can say.

A shepherd's lot is 'eavy,
An' a shepherd's lot is poor
In every kind o' weather you can think of –
An' some more!
They works by night an' day –
Why, it's enough to make yer weep!
If you ask me, a shepherd's
Just as silly as 'is sheep. . . .
I likes to eat, I likes to drink,
I likes to lie a-bed;
I calls no man *my* master –
'Ere's what I do instead:
I nicks a little chicken
Or I bags a side o' beef,
So guard yer goods when I'm about
Because I am a *thief!* . . .
No ducks that quack
Are safe from Jack,
Nor any sow that squealed;
Nor any sheep or lamb that's left
Unguarded in the field.
And O, but it's a lamb this night
On which I've got me eye –
I liked the black and white of it
As I went passing by.
An' so among the rocks I creep,
An' opens up me sack . . .
[*Very faint bleat of a lamb.*]
An' slips the lambkin in–
[*Slightly louder bleat.*]
Now!
It belongs to Thieving Jack!

[*Bleat.* THIEVING JACK *chuckles. Bell begins to sound
midnight.* SHEPHERDS *play and sing on the hill.*]

BEN: [*sings*] Now the bell at midnight
Chimes to make us glad,
Bringing in the birthday
Of a shepherd lad.

JOHN: [*sings*] He shall have a wooden crook,
A smock as clean as light;
He shall have a lambkin
Whose wool is black and white.

[*Bell ceases striking. Light begins to grow in
the sky above the* SHEPHERDS.]

DAN: [*alarmed*] Good father, and grandfather dea[r]
What is that light, I pray,
That burns above us in the sky
And turns the night to day?
Each spike of grass, each stone, is bright
Upon the midnight hill —
Yet lamb and sheep they soundly sleep,
And silent are, and still.

JOHN: [*gazing up, wondering*] Such fire it comes not
from the stars,
Nor comes it from the moon —
And bolder is it than the sun
That blazes at the noon.

BEN: My children, kneel;
My children, pray
That God may give us grace,
For none may know when he must go
To meet him face to face:
[*Music.*]
Here is a holy place.

[*Music. More light. Three* ANGELS *appear in the sky above
the summit of the hill. Music behind the following:*]

1ST ANGEL: Fear not, shepherds, for I bring
Tidings of a new-born King –
Not in castle, not in keep,
Nor in tower tall and steep;
Not in manor-house or hall,
But a humble ox's stall.

2ND ANGEL: Underneath a standing star
And where sheep and cattle are,
In a bed of straw and hay
God's own Son is born this day.
If to Bethlehem you go,
This the truth you soon shall know.

3RD ANGEL: And as signal and as sign,
Sure as all the stars that shine,
You shall find him, shepherds all,
Swaddled in a baby-shawl;
And the joyful news will share
With good people everywhere.

2ND ANGEL: Therefore, listen as we cry:

THREE
ANGELS: Glory be to God on high,
And his gifts of love and peace
To his people never cease.

[*Light and music fade on* ANGELS. *A moment of silence. The* SHEPHERDS, *bewildered, shake their heads, rub their eyes.*]

DAN: Grandfather, O tell me clear,
Did *you* see and did *you* hear
Angel-voices, angel-gleam?
Do I wake? Or do I dream?

BEN: [*reassuring*] Why, indeed the angels came . . .

93

JOHN: [*quickly*] And I heard and saw the same . . .

BEN: So, with swift and fearful tread,
         Let us to that cattle-shed.

DAN: But the night is dark and deep.
         Who will watch the lambs and sheep?

BEN: Dearest grandson, do not fear;
         God will keep them safely here:
         Guard the hill and guard the plain
         Soundly till we come again.

         [*He smiles, and removes the pot from the fire.*]

JOHN: Then let's music play . . .
DAN: And sing!
BEN: For we go to greet a King!

         [*Music of the* SHEPHERDS *is heard as they
         approach.* JOSEPH *stands at the entrance to the
         stable to greet them.*]

JOSEPH: I bid you enter, shepherds . . .
         My name is Joseph.
         Out of Nazareth
         I journeyed far with gentle Mary here,
         And who, this night, a son has borne so dear.
         Therefore, good shepherds from the mountain
            steep,
         Draw near to where the infant lies asleep
         That you may tell to all, and tell it true,
         The tale of wonder now made known to you.

BEN: [*shaking him by the hand*] Joseph, we thank
            you for your welcome warm
         As we step in from out the weather's harm. . . .

94

No gift have I to bring the Heavenly King
Save my poor fiddle, and a fiddle-string.
[*He kneels.*]
But this, that is my comfort and my joy,
I freely offer to the Holy Boy.

JOHN: And I, sweet mother, as the babe I scan,
And see God's gift to woman and to man,
Give him my whistle-pipe.
[*He kneels and offers it to* MARY.]
Now, haste the day
As a good shepherd, *he* will pipe and play.

DAN: [*steps forward*] Jesus, I bring a greeting fair
            and fine,
Proud that your birth day is the same as
            mine.
Alas, no gift have I in either hand,
I've neither gear nor goods at my command:
Only this drum.
[*He kneels.*]
But with the crowing cock
I'll have a shepherd's crook, a shepherd's
            smock;
Yet these I will not bring, but with the light,
My dearest gift – a lambkin black and white.
This I am promised. This is to be mine –
And mine to give: and of my love, a sign.
The lamb I'll offer, for your keep and care,
On bended knee, to mark the day we share.

[THIEVING JACK *is now standing on his own.*]

THIEVING JACK: [*to audience*]
Great blocks and bricks,
Now 'ere's a fix –
An' all of me own makin'!
If truth I tell,
To prison-cell
A journey I'll be takin'!
For 'ere I am,
That little lamb
Snug in me thievin' sack . . .
[*Pause. Then he comes to a decision.*]
BUT
I'll be strong
An' shame the wrong,
An' dare to give it back.
This Infant King
Of whom they sing
Is merciful and good;
So, from this day,
As best I may,
I'll do things as I should!

[*He turns towards the* SHEPHERDS, MARY *and* JOSEPH *and kneels. Takes out lamb and offers it.*]

In small groups, try out your own ways of reading this verse play.
   As you read your part, think about the meaning of the words. Try to make it sound like conversation.

Find carols and poems that have the same message as this verse play.

Write your own story or poem called "The gift" to add to your collection.

Celebrate Christmas in your classroom by sharing part of this play and some of your own poems and stories.